JERRAD LOPES

MY DADDY'S HERO

ART BY
ADAM GRASON

HARVEST HOUSE PUBLISHERS
EUGENE, OREGON

Published in association with the literary agency of Wolgemuth & Wilson.

Cover design by Emily Weigel Design.
Interior design by Left Coast Design.

For bulk, special sales, or ministry purchases, please call 1-800-547-8979.
Email: CustomerService@hhpbooks.com

ᴍ This logo is a federally registered trademark of the Hawkins Children's LLC.
Harvest House Publishers, Inc., is the exclusive licensee of this trademark.

My Daddy's Hero

Text copyright © 2024 by Jerrad Lopes
Artwork copyright © 2024 by Adam Grason
Published by Harvest House Publishers
Eugene, Oregon 97408
www.harvesthousepublishers.com

ISBN 978-0-7369-8776-9 (hardcover)
Library of Congress Control Number: 2023945657

Printed in China

24 25 26 27 28 29 30 31 32 / LP / 10 9 8 7 6 5 4 3 2 1

Elijah, Eden,
Ella, and Emilia—
there is only one hero
worthy of your praise.

Did you know my daddy is a superhero?

He is big and strong.

My daddy creates forts
out of blankets . . .

... or even in a tree.

My daddy picks me up
high above his head
and carries me
on his shoulders.

My daddy takes broken things and makes them as good as new.

He even fixes my owies
when I get hurt.

My daddy knows how to protect me and keep me safe from scary things.

My daddy works hard to make sure we have food to eat and a warm place to sleep.

My daddy knows everything about me and loves me fully.

First Step

Mommy daughter date

Happy Birthday!

"Thank you for being my hero, Daddy!"

"You're welcome, sweetie. Did you know that Daddy has a hero too?"

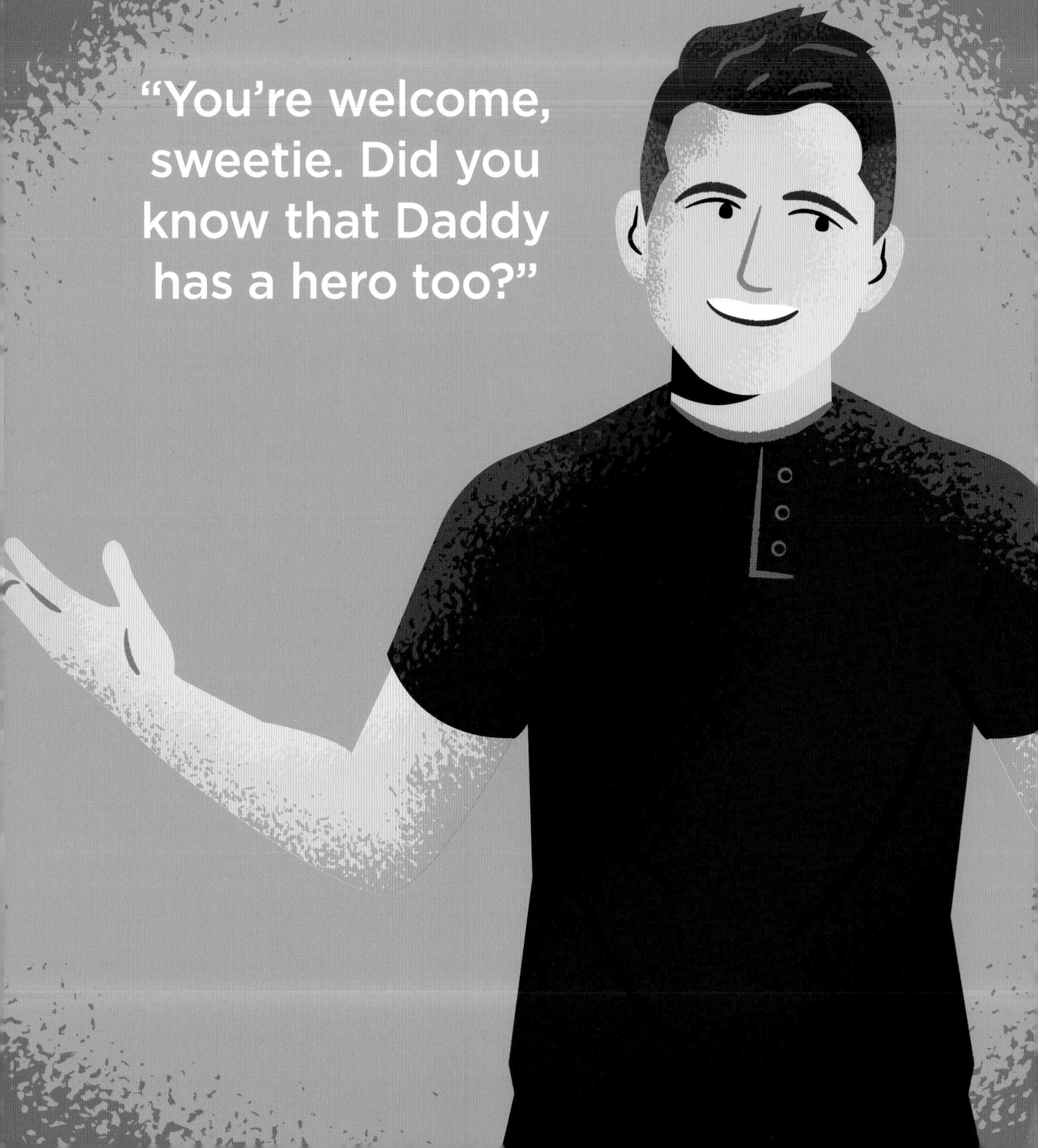

"Daddies have heroes?"

"Yes! They sure do!"

My hero is big and strong.

My hero built the mountains and filled the oceans.

He even put the stars and planets in place.

My hero is the answer

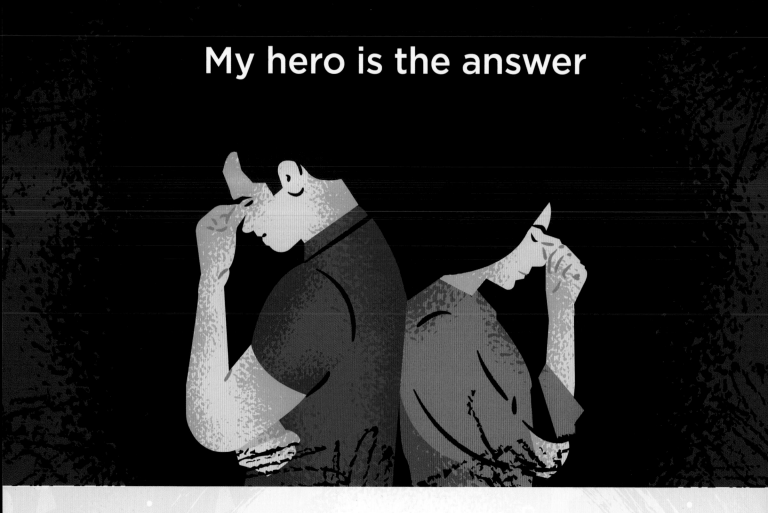

to the world's biggest problems.

My hero picks me up and carries me when I fall down.

My hero protects his family.

My hero takes care of us and makes sure we have everything we need. My hero knows everything about me and loves me fully.

"Wow! Who is your hero, Daddy?"

"My hero is Jesus."

He is the hero of our family and the hero of the whole world!

Jerrad Lopes is an author, a Christian pastor, and the founder of Dad Tired, a nonprofit ministry focused on equipping men to lead their families well. He hosts the weekly *Dad Tired* podcast, listened to by hundreds of thousands of men around the world. His books include *Dad Tired, The Dad Tired Q&A Mixtape,* and *Stop Behaving.* He and his wife, Leila, live in South Carolina with their four children.

Adam Grason is an illustrator and designer from Port Orange, Florida. He has been honored to work with clients like Disney, Target, Williams Sonoma, Google, Crossway, and more. Adam is a dedicated husband, father, and follower of Jesus.